THERAPY

Cover by DEATH

Photos by DR. DEATH
Assisted by THE DOCTOR'S ASSISTANT, NURSE MUERTE
Modeling by JUSTINE MCCLUSKEY/NURSE MUERTE

Produced from THE KING'S CHAMBER/
THE DOCTOR'S OFFICE

Produced at DARK MAN Inc. in Holly, Michigan

THERAPY

THE POEM BOOK

Mike McCluskey

Library of Congress Control Number: 2018903168
ISBN: Hardcover   978-1-9845-1354-0
               Softcover   978-1-9845-1353-3
               eBook   978-1-9845-1352-6

Print information available on the last page.

Rev. date: 03/19/2018

To order additional copies of this book, contact:
Xlibris
1-888-795-4274
www.Xlibris.com
Orders@Xlibris.com
773236

CONTENTS

PATIENT

ESCAPE

PATIENT

?

Open your eyes, your real eyes,
So you can realize,
Where the real lies,
Seeing the real lies.

Psychoanalysis

He has a severely disturbed mind,
Brought about by time,
In a world that tries and pries,
Inside grows despise,
Behind the reflection where his mind lies,
The blackest eyes,
He hasn't spoken a word in over thirty years; he writes,
He hasn't broken how he truly feels; his rights,
Staring at the wall; not seeing the wall,
They put up the wall; he sees through the wall,
He lives within his head,
Far beyond driven in your dread,
He always wears a mask, his true face is rarely seen,
Except in front of me,
In a strait jacket,
Simply acting placid,
My vision is much clearer,
Staring into the mirror.

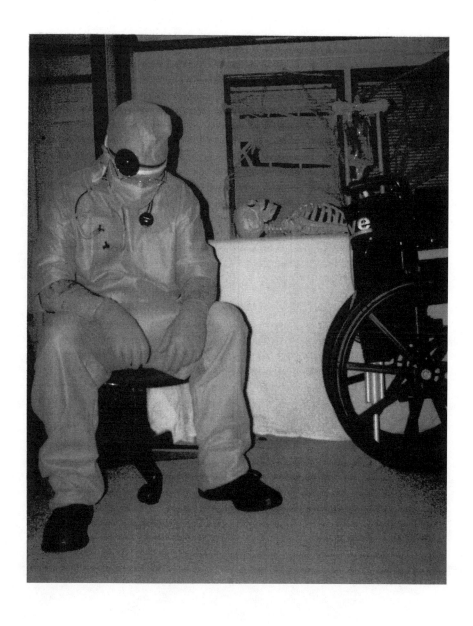

I Need Some Therapy

I want to quit again,
I feel defeated,
I feel cheated,
Up to my head in quicksand,
Never beheld a helping hand,
Freedom out of reach, but I can see it,
With constant distractions so I can't seize it,
Mission of the mistaken, once again taken,
I need some therapy,
To be a planted tree, blessing sent to me,
There I'm free,
A rose to be, but they just kill the seed,
Dare I be?
I need my pen to bleed instead of me.

PhD

Poetry-Honing darkness,
Poet conforming doctrines,
Psychologically Holding Death,
Psycho logically expressed,
Prescription penned in the doctor's office.

Mental Patient

Irritation,
Mental patient,
Impatient mentality,
Testing therapy,
Aggravation,
Mental patience,
Inpatient mentally,
Stressing therapy.

Medication

Therapeutic when I sharpen my knife,
When I say knife, I mean my pen,
Therapeutic when I take your life,
When I say life, I mean your mind's pen,
Therapeutic when I desecrate,
To decorate your thoughts and illuminate,
Therapeutic when I decimate,
Meaning to free your eyes and help create,
Therapeutic when I write with your blood on the walls,
Meaning ink to paper,
Therapeutic when I destroy the halls,
Meaning I won't allow your ability to think taper,
Therapeutic when I bury you whole,
Meaning I hide you from your foe,
Therapeutic when I take your soul,
Meaning I'll give you somewhere to go.

Therapeutic

You should thank God that this writing is therapeutic,
The mirror tells me to kill, but this is more prudent,
You're all lucky that I always resist,
Because God knows on how you always persist,
In your death wish of my wish,
You think my life is worth less,
But you're worthless but don't deserve death,
You deserve hell with worse left,
You should thank God that he saved my might,
You can hate writing, but it can help save lives,
You can hate me, you can hate my life,
But I hate life, for death I write.

Insane in an inane world,
In chains with no way to stir,
In rain with pain it blurs,
Sin reigns in flames incurred.

Trapped within the Inkblot

I don't need to see a shrink,
I am in the inkblot, I think?
I think,
So I'm always on the brink,
Of something,
Hopelessly struggling,
To be freed,
Something to be seen,
In the basement, see my feet dangling,
My body swaying from the strangling,
From the noose hanging, there I'll be,
Now that's therapy,
See me again in the inkblot,
When the ability to think stops,
When my body stinks and reeks rot,
I'll still reach out,
Even when you think doubt,
I'll blot out that weak route,
Find me again in the inkblot,
When in my casket they keep locked,
The oblong peace box,
Epitaph written on a shining rock,
When still the worms feed, letting greed out,
Still ink bleeds out,

Even when my ability to bleed stops,
The meek drop, but never does the ink stop,
Keep watch on the ink drops,
Trapped within the inkblot.

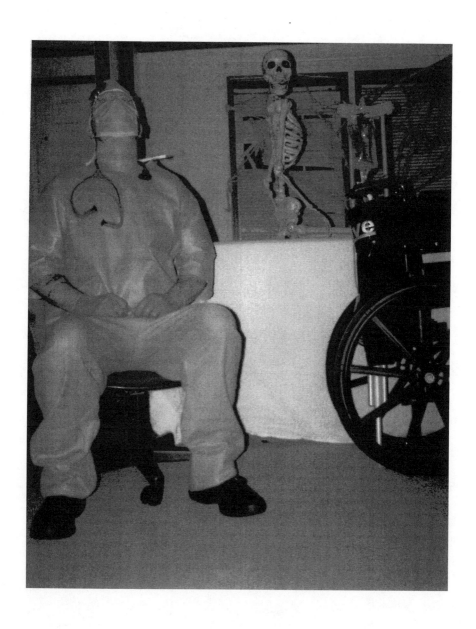

Doctor My Eyes

Eye surgeon,
War-wounded mental patient,
Already hurt but it's urgent,
No more patience, more patients,
Insert my eyes where yours were,
Bizarre works, you see what I see,
Thirty-some years worth,
Berserk and frightened, you can't handle the scene,
Look through my eyes,
And realize,
See my demise,
Through real eyes,
Doctor my eyes,
Wish I couldn't see at all,
Sewn from their lies,
Wish I couldn't feel at all,
The procedure engulfs you,
Shaking convulsions,
Only pain to hold you,
Hopeless in living nightmare implosions,
Am I a madman?
Evil solutions just surge in me,
How can damned man make me the bad man?
I am the curse in me; it's time for eye surgery,
Look through my eyes,
And realize,
See my demise,
Through real eyes,

Doctor my eyes,
Wish I couldn't see at all,
Sewn from their lies,
Wish I couldn't feel at all.

Death VII

I represent the dead and death,
Fog in every mustered breath,
From the land of graves,
With hopes to have your soul saved,
Raise my head from my hood when I hear pain,
Feel tension in my heart when I hear rain,
When my epitaph is read,
Feel my thoughts again,
I was lost, but now I'm found from doom,
The only light that found me was the light of the moon,
From my tomb arose,
A black rose,
Ugly and dark,
But still a light life in my heart,
A past of pain had made me stronger,
Passing any games that became harder,
When my epitaph is read,
Feel my thoughts again.

Life after Death

Life is the slow killing of you,
Therapy is accepting the slow building of truth,

Also known as death alight,
Also known as life,

Therapy teaches you to try to live,
Therapy is what your mind has left to give,

Life is simply only death-defying,
Therapy for me is death and dying.

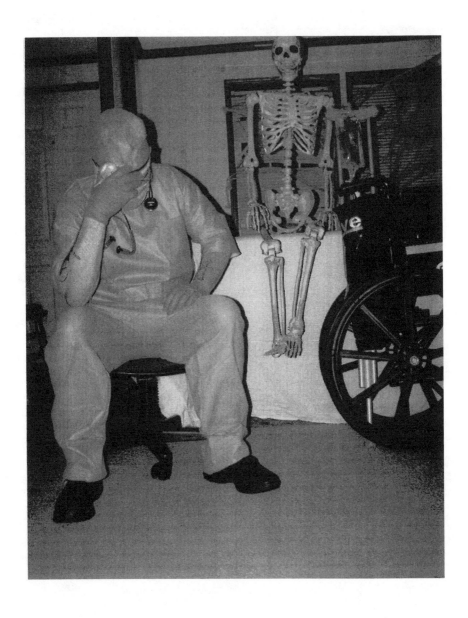

Egg Man

I walk around with egg on my face,
Egg all over the place,
But I'm the disgrace?
You all made the waste,
I must look stupid,
About to lose it,
I feel stupid,
They make me feel useless,
Faze me,
Shame me,
Hate me,
Until I'm made crazy,
Hazing as I coast,
I was just walking like a ghost,
For their own amusement with yolk they coat,
Embarrassed like a bare-assed jackass with no coat,
Ignored until they need a scapegoat,
Destroyed like a corpse at the end of pain's rope,
It's like I'm a ghost,
And everyone knows,
But I don't know,
I just normally go,
Smashed egg on my head,
Just amusement for them.

My Therapy

Sometimes I feel like I just can't deal
with the pressures of life,
Therapeutic with my rites,
With my right to pen,
Trapped within a pen,
From all the frustration that I've pent,
So I walk around with a bloody pen,
Stab it into my heart again and again,
Damned within this art again and again,
Jam it into my eyes,
Sadness brought with bloody cries,
Ram and stick it in my brain,
Madman with a pen insane.

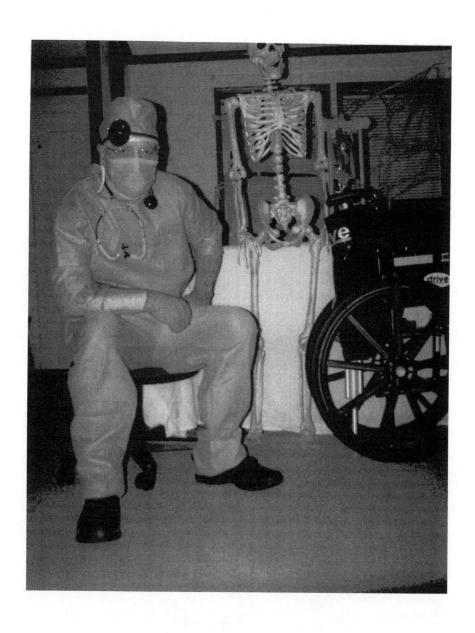

Nervous II

Tense and uptight,
Might of the nerves,
Disturbed with no words,
Curse to ignite,
Sight of my fight,
Height of paranoia observed,
Stir that's occurred,
Worst end of plight,
Like a manic panic,
Habit that must crush,
Rush with sweat added,
Tragic heart thrust bust,
Plus feeling disadvantaged,
Damaged and I'm nervous.

Why I Write

This is my own personal therapy,
Now I realize,
With my real eyes,
Not their blind guise disguised as helping me,
Now I see,
I don't even know where reality lies,
They've told me so many lies,
They've shown terrible therapy,
But they're not right,
That's why I write,
They don't have the right,
This is my rite,
Wave with their left hand and stab with the right,
That's why I write.

?
◇

What a cursed life I live,
Given everything I could give,
Any who don't like my depression expressions
should live the life I've lived,
In a world of sin doing a lifetime bid,
Sadness ever since I was a kid,
No matter what I did.

The Doctor Can See Me Now

Doctor, doctor, I need to make a visit,
The voices in my head say I'm schizophrenic,
Because I panic,
And when they start screaming, I can't stand it,
Wait a minute, I must be mistaken,
The doctor told me to listen,
To the voices and their wishes,
I was suspicious,
But I need this therapy,
Life I can't deal with; it's scaring me,
He said, "If they tell you to kill, then kill,
It will fulfill like a pill,
Drink from the blood spill,
Help a stirring will stand still,
If you can, it will,
Understand you're not ill,
There's just a void you need to fill,
So plan with skill."
He said if I get caught, then he's not here,
He'll disappear,
This is my own path to track,
He wrote a prescription for that,
"Kill two or three then call me if there's mourning,
We don't need a conscience forming."
Just then a stench arrived,
It smelled like something died,

Then to my surprise,
Right before my eyes,
It's my doctor, a severed head!
Sitting in his lap, grinning, staring dead ahead!

¿

You keep trying to fix Frankenstein,
While I'm dying,
Dead parts decaying,
Just a zombie remaining.

Am I Crazy or Creative?

The torn soul of an artist,
Honest where lies impress,
Now which side of the mirror is expressed?
Reflect on what reflects,
Make it even when they hate it,
Am I crazy or creative?
Insane or genius?
Trying to see with Jesus,
Discount feelings but they can be seen,
Feelings are powerful energy,
Imagine it forced onto paper,
Forged into paper,
Hardly able to contain it,
Am I crazy or creative?
Profound or odd?
Trying to bond with God.

Diagnosis

. . . Staring into the mirror,
I don't know how much of me is here,
In society, he can't hack it,
Keep him enraged in a strait jacket,
Regard him as not human,
Pure evil with intuition,
Why was he ever to be?
HE MUST NEVER BE SET FREE!

Out

Brains ripped out,
They drip out,
Blood drains out,
Insane rout,
When thoughts hang out,
They drag out,
Like when trees of the forest shout,
About dead bodies along the route,
From the forest floor they're growing out,
The dead past showing out,
Rain clouds flowing out,
Brain storms pouring out,
Black reign like tears stain out,
My veins to my pen is the weather vane's out.

Patient Escape

You made me doubt,
Contemplate my own cause,
You all were right; they should have never let me out,
I am the evil monster that you thought I was.

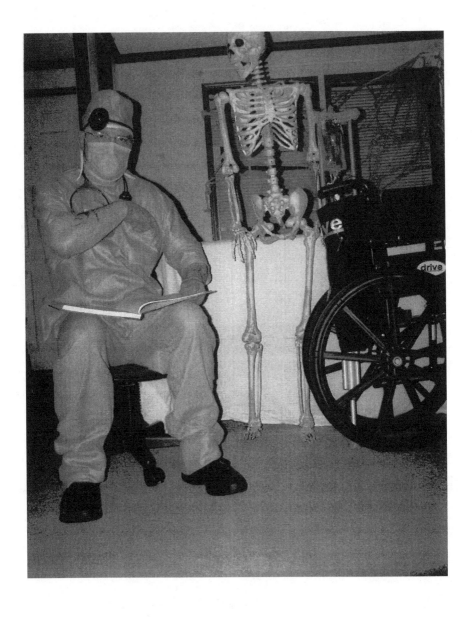

Therapy

My own personal therapy,
A pad and a pen,
Madman in a pen,
Unleash to a dead piece of tree,
I always listen to me,
Psychology penned,
From the mirror what was pent,
My own personal therapy,
Put into paper,
Dead thoughts or dead flowers,
Burn the eraser,
Ascend away or dread powers,
Cure exhaler,
Ink as smoke to extend hours.

Patience Is Death

Patience is death,
Slow decay of the heart,
Waiting at your own wake until there's nothing left,
Wading in life's wake until it drifts you apart.

ESCAPE

GRIM

GRIM

Chapter 1   Grim Life

His name was Grim; his life was grim,
He was submissive, and his wit was dim,
The butt of jokes again and again,
Dirty, ridiculed, but still managed to grin,
Bumbling and stuttering, people
would take advantage of him,
Balding and his remaining hair was thin,
He was missing teeth, short, hunchbacked and overweight,
With bosses overbearing, his soul scale bore overweight,
He worked all day and stayed late,
But when it came to payday, he was made to wait,
Grim worked for the circus, cleaning animal stalls,
Fall of a poor man but gave his all,
He always wanted to be a clown,
But held a frown, he was never allowed.

Chapter 2   Grim Death

Grim loved the circus,
He thought he found his purpose,
Even when he felt worthless,
His aspirations to be a clown made it worth it,
He wanted nothing more than to be a clown,
So he kept coming around,
By the promises of his bosses he was bound,
But they took advantage of every chance they found,
They paid him down sometimes and
convinced him somehow,
With lingering promises of being a clown,
So he started to hound,
They used him for years, now no longer wanted around,
Bosses wanted to avoid more payment, so
they just killed him oh so simple,
Tranquilizer dart to the temple.

Chapter 3   Grim Limbo

Grim's family hadn't seen him in years;
it seemed like ages ago,
They hated when he left home for a goal to follow,
They all lived in a mobile home, but he wanted to grow,
Go to work at the circus show,
He slept in animal stalls, in straw;
the bed his bosses showed,
It was all he would know,
Until they killed him though,
But his family missed him so,
The bosses warned them to let it go,
Or they would kill them slow,
Loved ones wouldn't let him go,
The dead didn't want him though,
So his soul was trapped in limbo,
Family wanted him because he was
good-hearted and helpful, so...

Chapter 4   Grim Revenge

Grim's family's loving will helped raise him,
From the depths it saved him,
But his brain had stayed grim,
They didn't want him dead, they wanted him to stay Grim,
The dead didn't want him because of
an evil unrest they sensed,
He emerged painting his face like a
clown to disguise his death,
Now he's altogether something else,
Digging up corpses as revenge for himself,
Digging by full moonlight,
Leaving dead bodies at the circus with delight,
Leaving nightmares with this fight,
Laying the dead in bed with his bosses at night,
Torment and murder by fright, from the dead his right,
Performing his revengeful rites.

THE END

Ghost Writer 2

A ghost that still writes,
Dead man that still fights,
Instilled rite,
It feels right,
I fill night,
Whether wrong or right.

Michael Myers

Inhumanly patient,
Biding my time,
This rage that I'm faced with,
Is rising inside,
Any good part in me died,
Long ago,
A murderous mind can no longer hide,
I can no longer cope,
There is no more hope,
I'm burning within,
My conscience is choked,
My knife is my friend,
This is not my end,
It's yours,
Awaiting revenge,
To even the score,
When blood drains, it pours,
Life was never fair to me,
Waiting the course,
And just think, this IS my therapy.

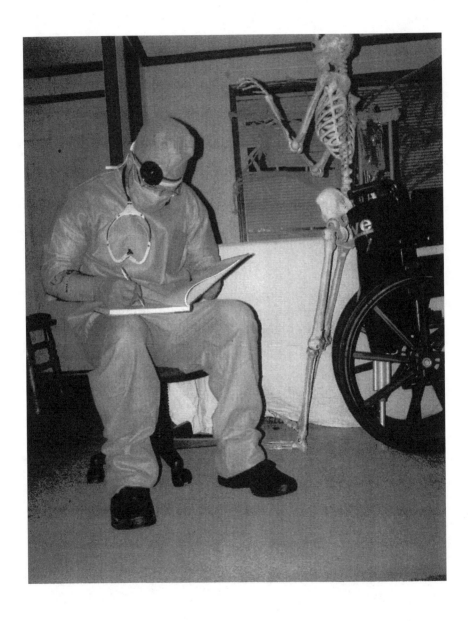

<u>My Poetry</u>

The insane ravings of an absolute lunatic,
The inane cravings of a doomed one who is sick,
Mental creativity pushed into a room with no view,
Mental therapy groomed in a tomb with a view askew,
Escape the state of the waste that awaits,
Escape of a wraith to replace his former shape.

Dark Man Ink

I slit my wrist to see if I can feel still,
Then I dip the quill in the spill,
Ink the pages with my blood,
I've always been misunderstood,
I will still leave my stain,
Open up your brain,
With the scars on my wrist to prove I'll try again,
And then I'll die again,
But then just to live through,
Despite you,
Might threw to fight fools,
I write truth to ignite you,
I had bled, now raise the dead,
When you read,
Strip your flesh from bone,
Groans grow in dark poems,
With the scars on my wrist to prove I'll try again,
And then I'll die again,
But then just to live through,
Despite you,
Open your mind to unbury me,
Resurrect me from the cemetery,
The epitaphs that laugh,
Carve my pain onto slabs,
Pour out my soul and wait for your pull,
And then sign my name onto your skull,

With the scars on my wrist to prove I'll try again,
And then I'll die again and again,
But then just to live through,
Despite you.

Mental Patience

I'm impatient,
But patience is life,
I'm a patient,
With no rights,
So I write,
So I don't stay dense,
With no light,
So how can I make sense?
With pad and pens,
No one else to hear my plight,
Hoping we stay friends,
When performing my rites.

Exorcism

I write instead of killing you,
Spoken softly but it's drilling you,
I'm living off Adrenalin,
Need an exorcism or my head will spin,
The exorcist when I'm writing this,
The demons in me I'm fighting with,
Need release from the hellish reign,
Free release from my pain it drains,
Sweet relief like blood is the ink it stains,
We release; the beast seeps onto our page.

The Shape

The shape,
The shadow the moon makes,
The hate,
Created by your rude ways,
The face,
Erased like a doomed wraith,
The state,
Kept in a renewed grave,
The fate,
Cursed to what the rules say,
I am . . .
The shape,
Formed from the black mist,
I stand,
Lifted with madness in blackness,
I can,
Withstand and expand when still in sadness,
I plan,
Under a mask when it's blackest,
I am . . .
The shadow the moon makes,
The shape.

Wicked Clown

Paint my face with your splattered blood,
Paint my face like a wicked clown,
Bloody tears and a crimson frown,
Bloody murder mural where I stood,
Drinking every bit of it that I could,
Digging in your chest until the heart is found,
Warm to the bite but it no longer pounds,
Eating the entrails, the mirror said I should,
The circus show is here,
I popped your balloon,
Laughing as I jeer,
On a unicycle I zoom,
Juggling organs while I steer,
All by the light of the moon.

Brain Surgery

I don't understand how your brains work,
An insane irk,
Your lame birth,
Inane worth,
Your quirks are laughable,
Oh, who to pass the scalpel to?
Enter Dr. Death,
Hold your breath,
It's me!
I've been missing,
But escaped again,
Back for a mission arisen,
Make the incision,
Cut along the scalp to begin,
Slice until I hit skull,
My eyes are aglow,
Rip open the skull slow,
Pull the sack back for brains to expose,
Stab and hack like I know what I'm doing,
Consume some for pursuing,
I might be evil,
Just trying to understand you people,
The humans I tried to study,
But all I did was get my hands bloody.

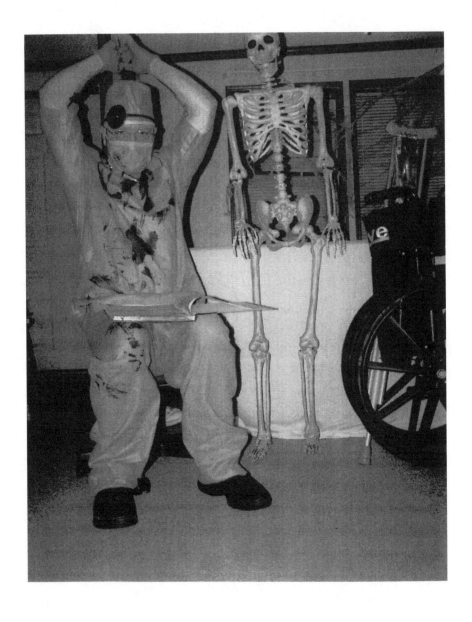

?

Therapy,
Enter me,
Bury me,
In the seed,
Clarity,
In the weed,
Dare I be?
In the tree,
Dare I breathe?
Free indeed,
Into me,
Therapy.

<u>Serial Killer</u>

Somebody must stop me,
I cannot stop myself,
Another dead body copy,
I drain out mental health,
Knife with my pen,
Ink stab stains like blood's pain,
Pent in a pen,
Penned rage from a brain's pang,
Maintain the read blood red rum murder,
Curb the surge of the urge,
The cursed stir of a cursor,
Incur a cure with the purge,
Writing in my test,
Killing off the stress.

Cyborg

Mirror call, miracle,
My call, Michael,
Motor cycle,
Circle of life on a motorcycle,
Automatically mobile,
No automobile,
The vehicle,
All be it killed,
More mechanical,
Mechanism instilled,
A machine's will,
Yet I breathe still.

Egg Man 2

My whole damned life I've been egg man,
Yolk soaked on my head again and again,
They did it as kids,
They did it back when,
No reason,
Just to look at him,
Madman they created,
Villain shamed and hated,
They made it,
I wanted to be a hero, but it faded.

Exhume to Read, Read to Exhume

Biding my time with a pen,
From within a pen,
Unleash all that I've pent,
With every word that I penned,
Under a mask feeling phantasmic,
Turn open the cover to unmask it,
Flip the pages, nothing too drastic,
Reading the words is like opening a casket,
Unwrap the mummy intact,
Brush back cobwebs, and skim within the grim tact,
A dim life held together by a thin tack,
Unfold to absorb and interact.

True Love

True love,
Renewed sun,
Return from when gloom won,
Then when we had knew none,
But new love is a bloomed bud,
Two seeds into one sum,
Some love can thaw the cold paths,
Withdraw the whole past,
When we hold hands,
Being so glad,
From a first kiss to a first wish,
Hugging and touching in preferred bliss,
From love inside,
Lover's eyes,
Love, it binds; love is blind,
Lovers try; lovers sigh,
Miss each other when we're not together,
A deep friendship to gather,
We always want to be together,
For bonding warmth to gather,
Love in me is therapy,
In a heartless world that is daring we,
Daring you with glaring truth,
True love it soothes,
Love you and love too,
See our true selves, love true,
You love and two love,
Show our true self, true love.

Schizophrenic

The feeling is getting bigger,
The urges are getting stronger,
Surging for me to falter,
Ignoring it makes them hinder,
Try to break free, but it lives here,
Feeding on my hunger,
Illuminating my wonder,
The emptiness, empty nest filler,
I must kill!
For the demons in me,
Fulfill the will!
It's devouring me,
I have to kill!
To find relief.

The Reason That I Wrote

For my own sanity,
For your very safety,
This is my therapy,
Where I can be,
Where I can see,
Where I can breathe,
Where I can find peace,
Find relief from grief,
So I don't kill you,
Let known the real truth,
So I don't kill myself,
Let it be known how I felt,
The only way that I can find hope,
The only way that I can cope,
This is the realest that I ever wrote,
The reason that I wrote.

The Goat

Point the finger,
That's the bad guy,
It just figures,
Sad guy into mad guy,
Your self-comforting accusations,
No other reason why,
Trade worthlessness for deflation,
Nice try,
The scapegoat,
The goat,
Someone to unjustly punish,
Pay the ultimate price,
The murder of innocence,
With no sense, you destroy life,
My rites, you're too weak, you never could,
Turn wrong into your right,
I die for your greater good,
Nice life,
The sacrificial goat,
The goat,
The lost ghost,
Caused by your false hope,
The one, the host with the most,
The last hope,
With the words that I wrote,
The one with the most hope,
Nevermore goes the quote,
The free crow among the cults,
The greatest of all time,

The goat,
A legend, breathing or dead,
Writing until and after the end,
When I die, you'll see,
There is no stopping me,
The last of my kind,
The greatest of our time,
The Greatest Of All Time,
The goat.

Trapped within the Inkblot Part 2

Trapped within the inkblot,
You've got to let me out,
Set me free!
By reading me!
Let my demons breathe!
They're devouring me!
They're screaming!
I thought I was dreaming!
Let loose the rage,
Open up my cage,
Read the pages,
Set the stages,
This page I'm made with,
This phase I stay with,
I'm here within,
Please let me breathe again!
EXORCISE!
REVEAL MY MIND!
EXHUME MY SKULL!
EXPOSE MY SOUL!

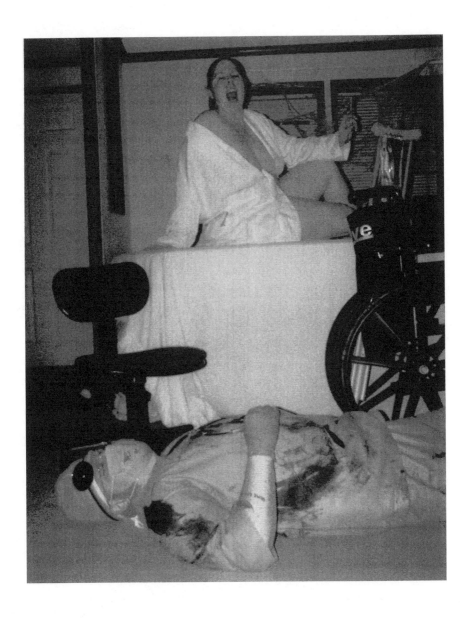

Prescription

I left a line for you to follow,
Let's see if your souls are too hollow,
You need to run but you waddle,
Try to keep your head out of the bottle.
Or will you wallow,
Knowing we're not granted tomorrow?
The dread drive leaving a scowl,
Leading me to howl,
You're so sordid, so you don't allow,
The sort of soul that you hobble,
My dead line through time carved in cobblestone to follow,
Until the deadline of time swallows.

November 1st

Where is my therapy?
Nothing left for me apparently, no empathy,
How can you smile in my face so carefree,
Knowing you really don't care for me,
Pushed into depression,
Crushed, depressed into the earth again,
Left with no worth again,
Just make me feel worse again,
I don't ever want to feel like I did that day,
How could you make me feel that way?
The day after,
The gray chapter,
You praise disaster,
In gay laughter,
It's black-and-white and clear to me to see,
You hate me greatly to deflate me,
Try to shake me because you didn't make me,
Then have the nerve to try to shape me,
I don't ever want to feel like I did that day,
How could you make me feel that way?
Now when I don't laugh, you have the gall to ask, why?
Yesterday you just passed by,
Chastise when I let my anger and hurt rise,
Blurred lines where utter hate and disregard lies,
So formulate your lies,
Form fake smiles, and practice wide eyes of surprise,
Today is all about you,
There is no yesterday; it's all about you,
I don't ever want to feel like I did that day,

How could you make me feel that way?
I don't even want to try,
I just want to die,
I just want to say goodbye,
I just want to die,
I can see but wish I couldn't see at all,
I can feel but wish I couldn't feel at all,
I feel it all; the sorrow grows,
You made today, no therapy; there is no tomorrow,
I don't ever want to feel like I did that day,
How could you make me feel that way?

Countdown to Extinction

Countdown to extinction,
I'm on the brink again,
I need to think again,
Let my own life plan expand,
Take back my own fate,
Shake up for my own sake,
Break up your foundation shape,
It always felt more like rape,
Therapy,
They rape me,
Therapy,
Break free,
Before they break me,
Before they waste me,
This is not suicide,
It's resurrection of the mind,
This is not suicide!
It's resurrection of the mind!
Intuition when I think,
Remember me when I'm extinct.

Foreshadowing

Peel back my foreskin,
Open into your forehead, it's forced in,
Hide your kin,
Hi, I'm beside your kid,
I am not your friend,
I used to pretend,
So now I expose myself, a damned man,
My writing has only just been the
insane ravings of a madman,
There is no one scaring me,
I'm only preparing for when you're daring me,
Freddy Krueger, the molester,
Feeling out your mind; the thought tester,
Test you because you test me,
The whole world is used to molesting me,
My therapy varying,
No rest in peace for me, not even when you bury me.

¿

A hardworking man damned,
With words from the heart,
In a planet that won't understand,
With this forgotten art,
Plans that won't grow,
Trapped in a design,
Seed that grows but slowed,
In the ashes of a mind.

COMING
HALLOWEEN 2017

AMERIKAN
NIGHTMARE:
SUPPOSEDLY
A DREAM

THE POEM BOOK

Other Poem Books by Mike McCluskey

"Patience Is Life"

2003

"F.T.W."

2004

"The Morgue"

2004

"What If..."

2005

"Book Of Rhymes"

2010

"Wicked"

2011

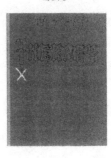

"Patience Is Life"

"Collector's Edition"

2013

"Therapy"

2016

Coming
Friday the 13th
January   2017

The 365 poem epic tome!
A ghost's journey continues!

JOURNEY 3009
THE POEM BOOK

...A Ghost's returning journey
to the other side and fighting
His other side... the dark side

Formed of twelve separate chapters
$6 each

Available on
Blurb.com

Follow a ghost's *journey* through the afterlife!

JOURNEY 3003

JOURNEY 3005

JOURNEY 3007

Edwards Brothers Inc.
Ann Arbor MI. USA
April 2, 2018